SPONSOR'S PREFACE

This is Guinness PLC's third year as a sponsor of the Royal Academy Summer Exhibition. Once again we are proud to be associated with an event of such calibre.

Both Guinness and the Royal Academy are leaders in their respective businesses. The Academy's Summer Exhibition is known internationally for its excellence and innovation in the field of contemporary art. Guinness PLC is one of the world's leading drinks companies for which excellence and innovation are a way of life.

Guinness has a long history of sponsorship of the arts. Recent sponsorships include the Scottish Ballet, the Lyric Theatre in Hammersmith, London and the Royal National Theatre. The company has, since its inception in 1759, built up an extensive collection of paintings, prints and sculpture, including Landseer's *Monarch of the Glen* and Raeburn's *The MacNab*.

Guinness likes to play an active part in encouraging new talent and will again be presenting the Guinness Prize to the best first-time exhibitor at the Summer Exhibition. This has been awarded in the past two years to Elpida Georgiou and Michael Westley.

The Royal Academy Summer Exhibition is one of the foremost attractions of the summer arts calendar in the UK. Guinness is delighted to be once again supporting this prestigious event.

Tony Greener
Chairman, Guinness PLC

Non ragioniam di lor, ma guarda e passa *
Tout passe – L'art robuste / Seul a l'éternité, / Le buste / ⌐

ROYAL ACADEMY
ILLUSTRATED 1993
A SOUVENIR OF THE
225TH SUMMER
EXHIBITION

In association with
GUINNESS PLC

Cover illustrated by Sonia Lawson RA

All dimensions are given in inches,
height precedes width

* The critic's view.
  Dante: Inferno, Canto III. 'Let's not discuss
  them, merely glance and pass by.'
  Translation by Tom Phillips RA
† The Academy's view.
  Gautier: L'Art.
  'Art alone, robust
  achieves eternity;
  the bust
  outlives a city turned to dust.'
  Translation by HWK Collam

Sir Roger de Grey KCVO, PRA
The Dog Walk
Oil 49 × 40

FOREWORD

There is a defiant outrageousness about the Summer Exhibition. Almost every other venue of contemporary art has become a fashion house, an austere temple of orthodoxy where we are shown only what is deemed at the moment to be curatorially correct. The rich variety of art is everywhere denied: only the Academy gives, each year, in painting, sculpture and architecture, the broader picture.

It is by their attendance in such great numbers that people announce their need and assert their democratic right to know what is going on in the visual arts. Only here can they be reminded so forcibly that great traditions are alive and flourishing: fine landscapes and portraits are still painted, the less modish kinds of abstraction thrive, the still life lives, romance is not dead, post-modernism in architecture has its brave alternatives, eccentricity abounds, political issues still find painted voice, and many seeming backwaters of referential painting and sculpture patiently bide their time.

More sophisticated and more fearless than the critics (who annually wilt before abundance to become a feeble chorus of ritual complaint), the public enjoys the challenge of a show in which visitors can make their own selection and back their judgements against those of the pundits who, historically, have seldom been right.

Everyone will of course notice the blaze of new paintings by David Hockney, as well as the silent tribute paid, in the form of important groups of work, to Sir Sidney Nolan, Dame Elisabeth Frink and John Bratby, among the members who exhibit posthumously and for the last time. But, in between the Kitajs and the Paolozzis and the Norman Fosters, there will be found . masterpieces by the less well-known. One of the traditional delights of the Summer Exhibition for each individual is to find his or her special discovery. The RA Illustrated tries to provide the flavour of such a quest.

That this present exhibition is once again more stimulating and more international than the last is more than anything a testimony to the inspired presidency of Sir Roger de Grey, who retires this year. The presence, as in all his years of office, of vibrant new work by him is proof that the Royal Academy is not just a grand building housing an august institution, but a fellowship of professional artists under the presidency of an eminent practitioner. In that lies its independence and its strength.
T. P.

Opposite: view of the Hockney wall in Gallery II.
Page 25: detail of wall in Gallery IX.
Page 43: detail of wall in Small South Room.

Sir Eduardo Paolozzi CBE, RA
Road to the Isles
Bronze 13 × 27

Sir Eduardo Paolozzi CBE, RA
Drummond House Project
Bronze h 10

Sir Norman Foster RA
Theme Park
Model h 14

Martin Shortis
Mango Man
Etching 10 × 6

Arnold Machin OBE, RA
Jacob Wrestling with the Angel
Pencil and watercolour 7 × 8

Bill Jacklin RA
Two Men Talking, From 'The Coney Island Suite'
Softground etching and aquatint 12 × 10

John Duffin
Shorebound
Etching 12 × 8

R. B. Kitaj RA
Whistler Vs Ruskin
Oil 60 × 60

John Wragg RA
First Light
Bronze h 18

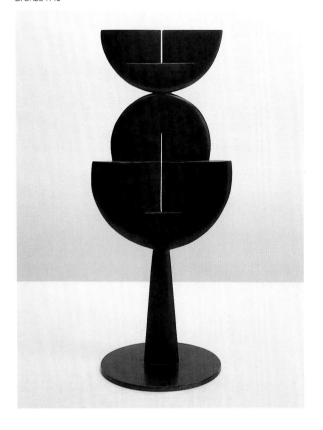

Willi Soukop RA
Abstract Image
Wood h 31

Bryan Kneale RA
Flamingo
Bronze h 26

Clive Barker
Vase with Flowers and Snail
Bronze h 15

Colin St. John Wilson RA
The British Library, Kings Library
Model (detail) h 33

Madeline Herbert
Stamford Wharf Development, South Bank (Architect: Lifschutz Davidson)
Model (detail) 70 × 74

Patrick Symons RA
Three Apple Trees
Pencil 25 × 35

Sarah Woodfine
Underside
Collagraph 9 × 12

The late Richard Diebenkorn Hon RA

Ocean Park Apt. 130

Oil 93 × 81

Nicholas Moore
Big Red Sarong
Linocut 43 × 32

Beverley Bennett
Untitled
Photograph 14 × 10

Michael Fell
Café in New York
Etching 15 × 15

Antonio Cattaneo
Volterra
Etching 10 × 8

Leonard McComb RA

Portrait of the Artist's Mother, Mrs Delia McComb

Oil 36 × 30

Barry Flanagan OBE, RA
Mexican Siren
Bronze h 14

Dhruva Mistry RA
Victoria Square Guardian – 2
Bronze h 17

John Davies
Lined Head
Epoxy resin h 23

Paul Huxley RA
Modus Operandi IX
Acrylic 39 × 39

Craigie Aitchison RA
Pink and Yellow Vase Still Life
Oil 12 × 10

John Hoyland RA
Twin Peaks 12.3.91
Acrylic 60 × 60

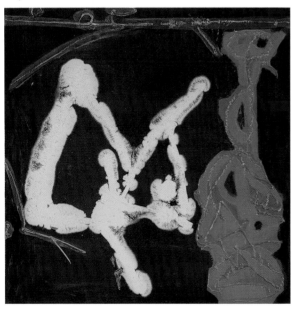

Jeffery Camp RA
Beachy Head
Oil on board 32 × 32

Bernard Cohen

Illuminations

Acrylic 72 x 72

Kit Surrey

The River

Graphite and conté on paper 25 × 39

Edward Cullinan CBE, RA (Edward Cullinan Architects Ltd)

Lycée Privé à Lagny - Perspective (Diploma Work)

Ink 21 × 21

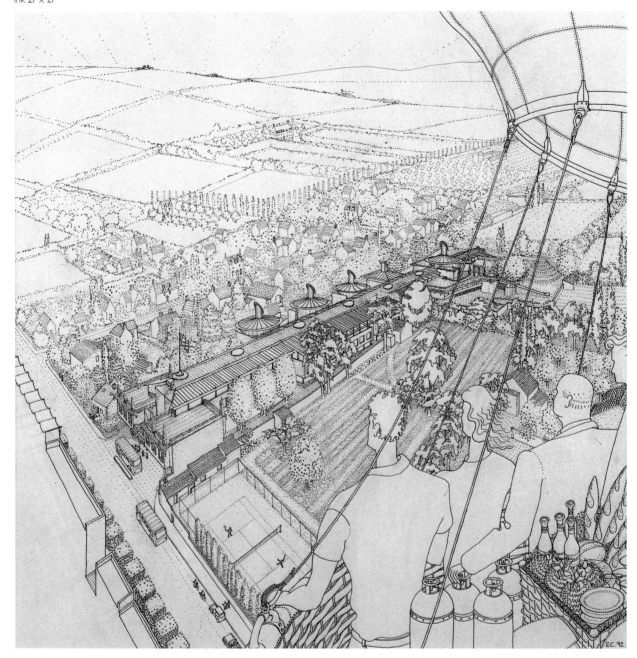

Sonia Hill
Jack the Lad
Oil 20 × 16

John Flint
The Flag
Oil 15 × 11

Stephen Goddard
Ann Shulver
Oil 15 × 9

Michael Kirkbride
Let's All Have a Disco
Tempera 8 × 7

Ceri House

Mr Blake, the Old Master of Pop Art

Mixed media 34 × 27

Mr Blake, the Old Master of Pop Art

Elizabeth Webb

Amadeus and St James

Oil 15 × 19

Francis Hill

The Good Old Days

Oil 17 × 21

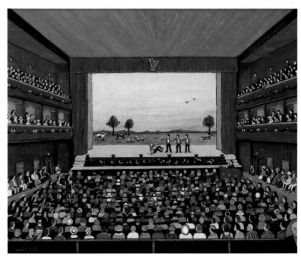

Gerald King

A Wrestling Bill for Peter Blake

Acrylic and collage 28 × 17

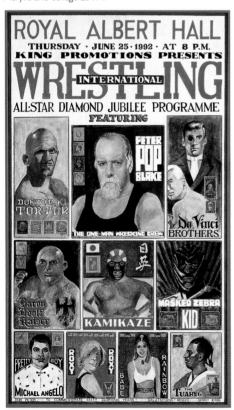

Gervase Elwes

The Demented Wife

Oil 22 × 34

Nahem Shoa
Self-Portrait
Oil 17 × 13

Jean Palmer
Head with Butterflies
Oil 7 × 6

Tai-Shan Schierenberg
Self-Portrait Small Head
Oil on zinc plate 9 × 6

Robert Clatworthy RA
Female Head II
Mixed media 14 × 11

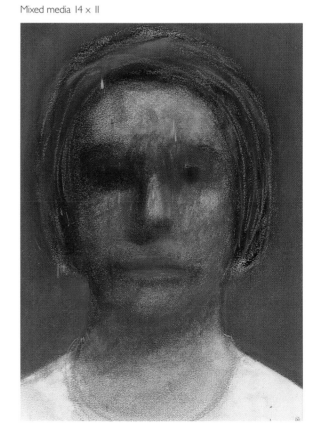

Tai-Shan Schierenberg
Portrait of a Waiting Woman
Oil 35 × 25

The late Sir Sidney Nolan OM, CBE, RA

Still Life Triptych

Oil, each panel 48 × 36

The late Sir Sidney Nolan OM, CBE, RA
Dog and Duck Hotel
Oil 38 × 48

The late Richard Eurich OBE, RA
Figures on a Beach 1979
Oil 21 × 31

Nicholas John Stirling Wordie

Internal Timber Structure of Salisbury Cathedral Spire

Model h 48

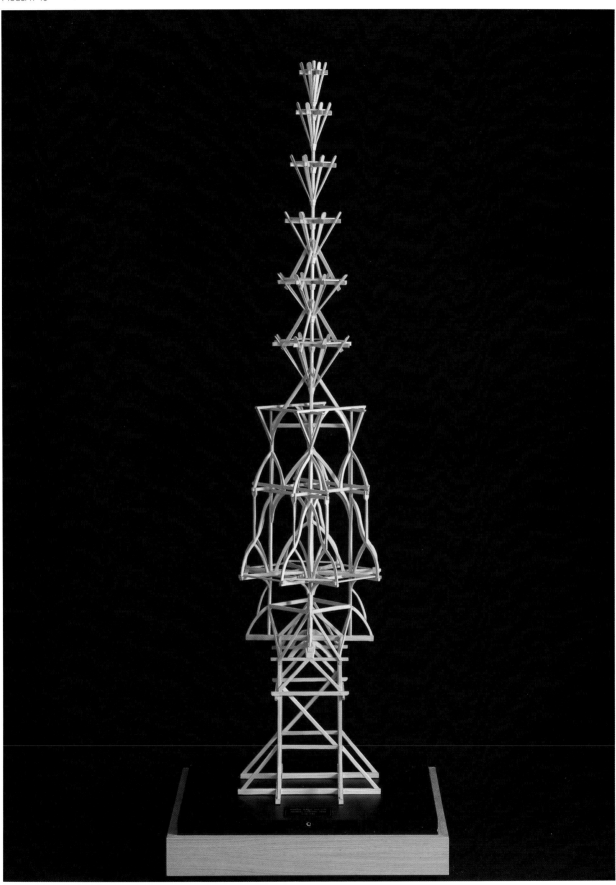

Sandra Blow RA
Sea Drift
Acrylic 88 × 123

Josef Herman OBE, RA
The Human Moment (Triptych)
Oil 51 × 113

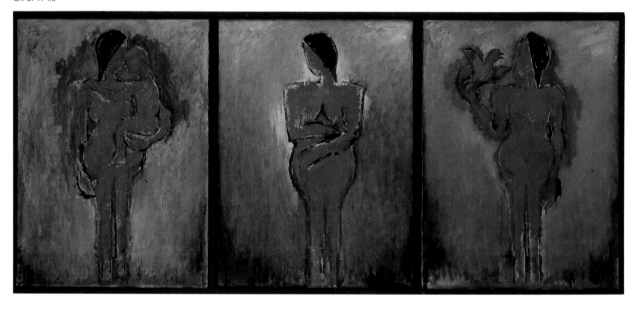

John Craxton

Cat, Bird, Tree

Oil 34 × 54

Timothy Hyman

Carnival Fragments

Etching and aquatint 8 × 23

Norman Ackroyd RA
South Cadbury Hill
Etching 22 × 30

Ben Johnson
Pool of Light
Screenprint 30 × 40

Robert Medley CBE, RA
a crucifixion
Oil 39 × 32

Martyn Baldwin
Well?
Oil 42 × 53

Birds Portchmouth Russum Architects
Morecambe Seafront
Ink 21 × 44

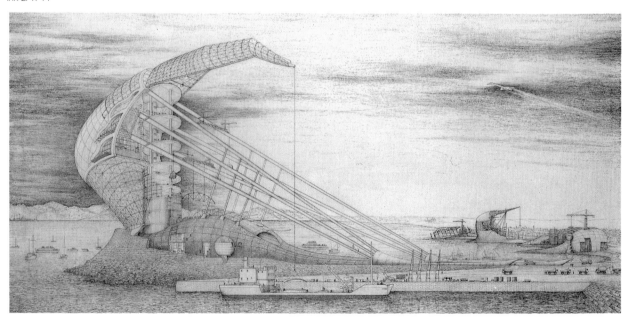

Sir Richard Rogers RA (Richard Rogers Partnership)
Futurum Diner
Model h6

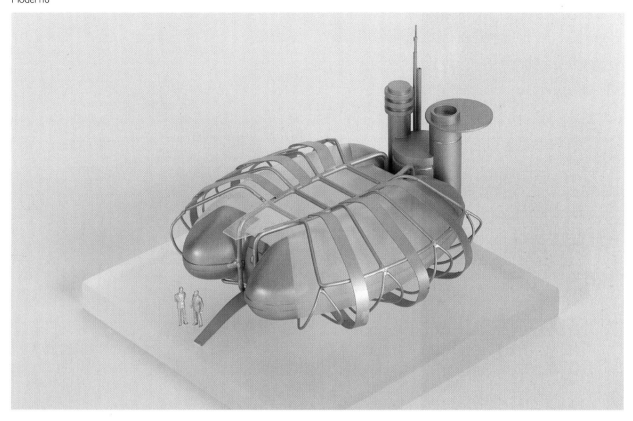

Sir Richard Rogers RA (Richard Rogers Partnership)
Futurum Diner
Model h6

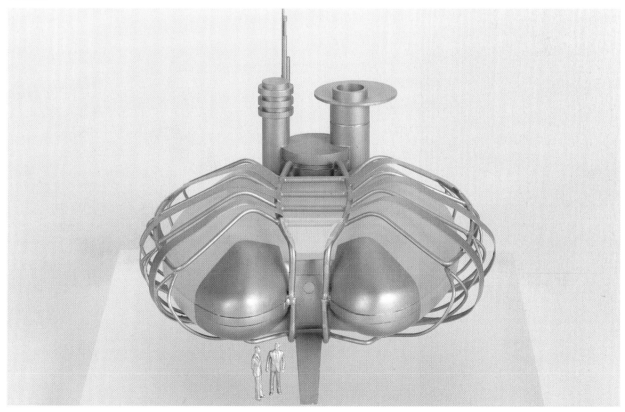

Wendy Pasmore

Untitled

Line and print 65 × 65

Eduardo Chillida Hon RA

Gravitation

Amate paper collage 16 × 15

Jasper Johns Hon RA
Untitled (#332)
Encaustic and sand 51 × 35

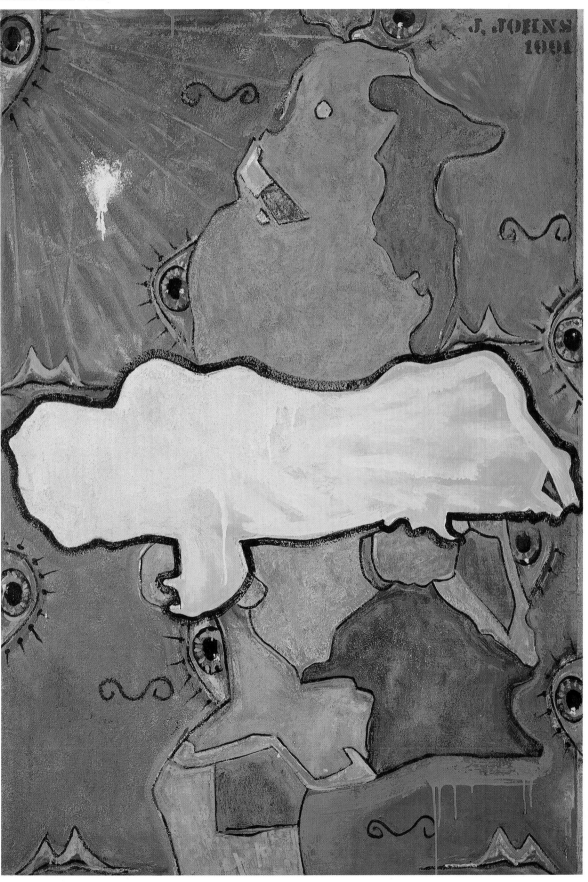

Frederick Gore CBE, RA
Incantation: Hibiscus and Red Sofa
Oil 40 × 30

John Titchell RA
Mid-Summer Day 7am
Watercolour (detail) 26 × 26

Philip Sutton RA
You Must be a Clown!
Oil 36 × 35

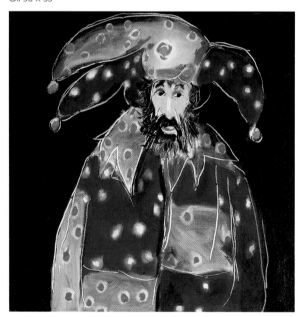

Donald Hamilton Fraser RA
Dodoni
Oil on paper 24 × 18

Charlotte Sorapure
Interior with Chair
Oil 31 × 21

Helen Lessore OBE, RA
The Birthday Cake
Oil 23 × 19

Colin Hayes RA
Fishing Boat, Amarinthos, Greece
Oil 29 × 39

Martin Leman
Voyage
Oil 11 × 15

Charles Hardaker
Waiting
Oil 11 × 9

**Detail of commemorative wall for
the late John Bratby RA in Gallery III**

The late John Bratby RA
Self-Portrait with Others
Oil 98 × 48

Ann Christopher RA
Out of Darkness
Bronze h 13

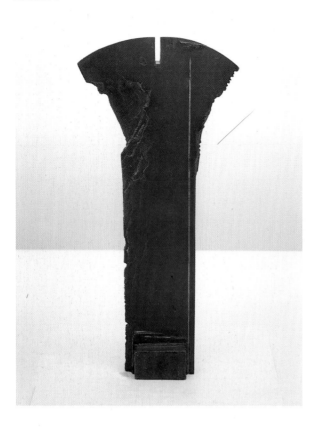

Sir Hugh Casson CH, KCVO, PPRA
Country Road near Amber
Watercolour 6 × 4

The late F.E. McWilliam RA
Symbiosis II
Bronze h 19

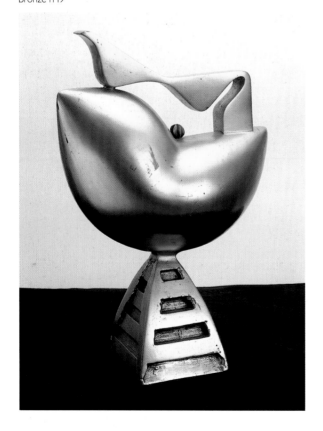

Helen Chadwick
I Thee Wed
Patinated bronze and fur h 10

Tim Mara
Can and Bowl
Screenprint 47 × 36

Norman Blamey RA
Study for 'The Harmonium'
Pencil 14 × 11

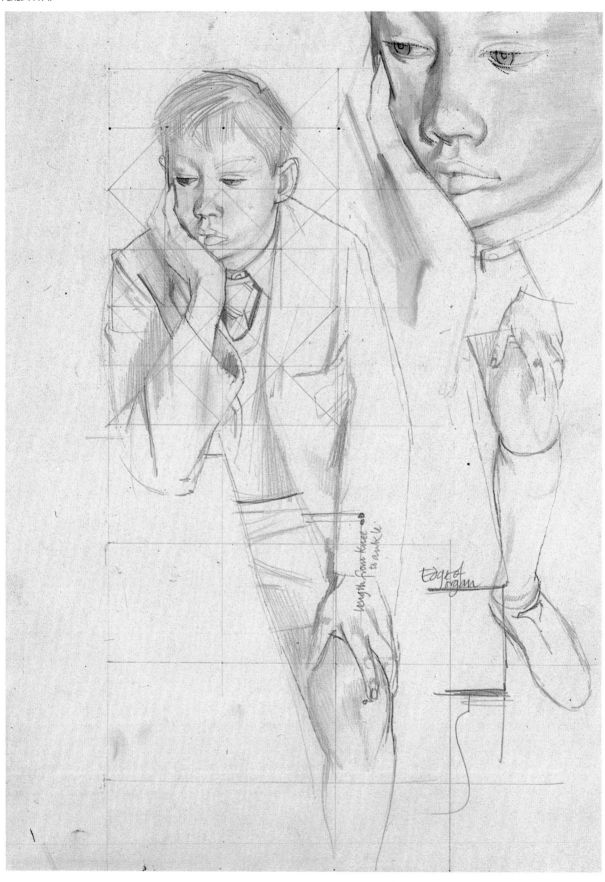

Tom Phillips RA
Salman R. as D.I.Y. Zola
Lithograph 15 × 11

The late Sir Robin Philipson PRSA, RA
Iconostasis
Oil 59 × 59

Gillian Ayres OBE, RA
Aquina
Oil d 96

Brendan Neiland RA
Free Flow
Acrylic 69 × 48

Ivor Abrahams RA
For a Time, For a Season I
Silkscreen and cutout 22 × 30

Jane Simpson
Kitchen Triptych
Photograph 20 × 20

Diana Armfield RA
Rio di San Moisé, Venice
Oil 11 × 8

Olwyn Bowey RA
The Artist's Greenhouse
Oil 32 × 40

Bernard Dunstan RA
Rehearsal, City of London Sinfonia
Oil 14 × 10

William Bowyer RA
Tuscan Landscape
Oil 39 × 49

The late Peter Greenham CBE, RA

Mrs Dorothy Hall 1960

Oil 20 × 16

Eileen Hogan
Lunch at Chelsea Arts Club with Carel Weight and Linda Sutton
Oil 35 × 47

Carel Weight CBE, RA
Helen Valentine, Curator, Royal Academy
Oil 15 × 17

John Bellany RA
Sunset Song
Oil 90 × 96

Karolina Larusdottir
The Secret
Oil 10 × 11

David Hockney RA
Still Life in Landscape
Oil 24 × 36

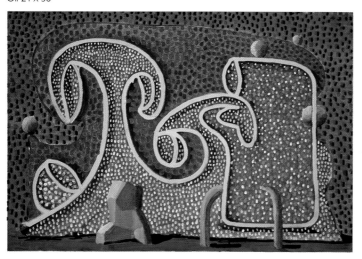

David Hockney RA
The Twelfth V. N. Painting
Oil 24 × 36

David Hockney RA
The Golden River
Oil 36 × 48

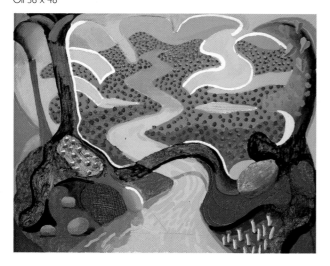

Still Life in Landscape
Oil 24 × 36

David Hockney RA
Esplanade
Oil 78 × 120

David Hockney RA
The Other Side
Oil 72 × 132

Geoffrey Clarke RA
No Title – Relief
Cast aluminium 25 × 16

Victor Pasmore CH, CBE, RA
The Eye and the Symbol
Spray and oil 95 × 48

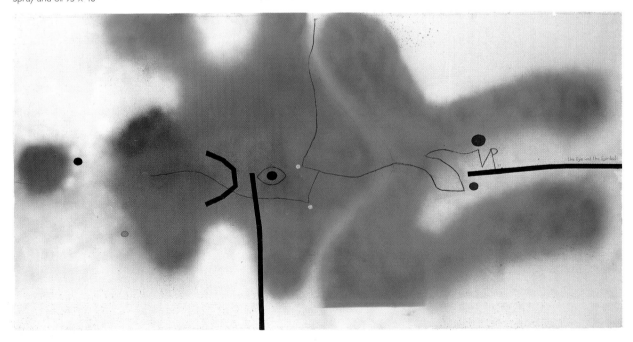

The late Sir James Stirling RA

Venice: Electa Bookshop in the Biennale Gardens

Ink and crayon 38 × 22

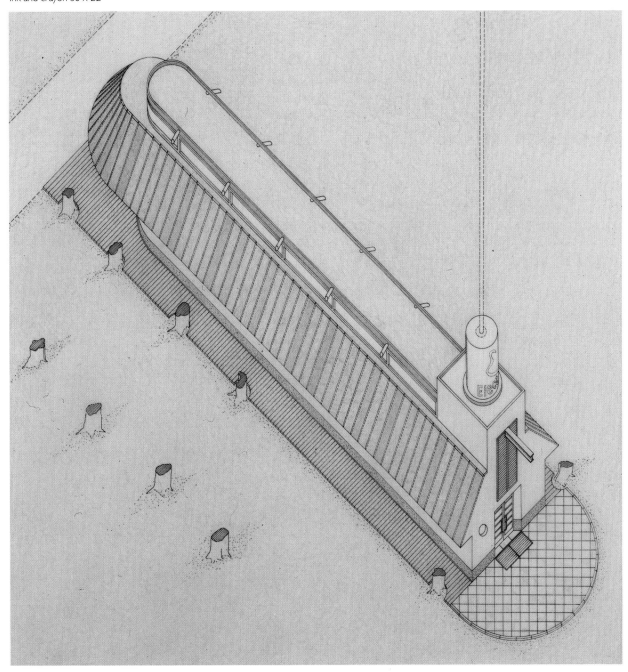

Paul Hogarth OBE, RA
Ponte Vecchio, Florence
Lithograph 22 × 17

Peter Freeth RA
Nocturne with Railway Bridges, Gospel Oak
Aquatint 18 × 24

Paul Koralek CBE, RA
Inner Harbour Study, Cardiff Bay
Pen 7 × 11

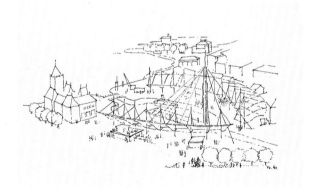

Anthony Green RA
Paradise
Oil d 103

Peter Howson
West Ham
Screenprint and woodcut 28 × 22

Gus Cummins RA
Triptych (St Mary) II
Gouache 41 × 65

Simon James
Dry Dock
Charcoal 40 × 45

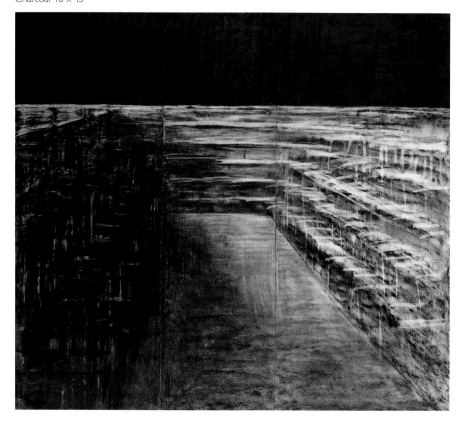

Peter Cook
Finchley Road Strands
Mixed media 31 × 47

Elizabeth Blackadder OBE, RA
Shrine, Kyoto
Watercolour 30 × 46

Adrian Berg RA
Stourhead, 25th June
Watercolour 9 × 13

Anthony Whishaw RA
Landscape II
Acrylic collage 47 × 120

David Tindle RA

Freesias in the Window

Egg tempera 18 × 16

Patrick Caulfield
The Second Glass of Whisky
Oil 24 × 30

Allen Jones RA
Untitled
Oil 22 × 20

Roy Lichtenstein
Interior with Shadow
Oil and magna 82 × 64

Stephen Chambers
Head of Eyes 1
Lithograph 32 × 24

Stephen Chambers
Head of Eyes 2
Lithograph 32 × 24

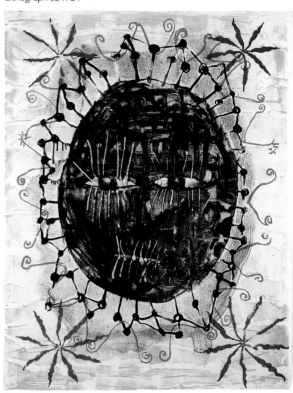

Terry Frost RA
Easter Fall
Oil and collage 72 × 48

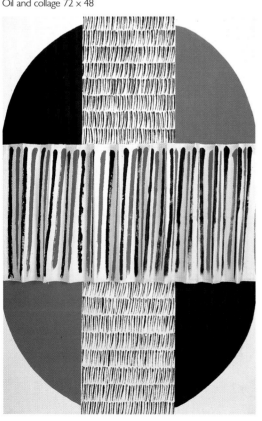

Anthony Salter
Edge of Darkness
Etching 7 × 5

**Installation shot of the Large South Room,
with John Maine's 'Pathway II'**

Paul Hawdon

Sky over the Aventine

Etching 20 x 27

Sasa Marinkov

Eastern Harvest

Woodcut 24 x 34

Noel Forster
Untitled
Oil 67 × 70

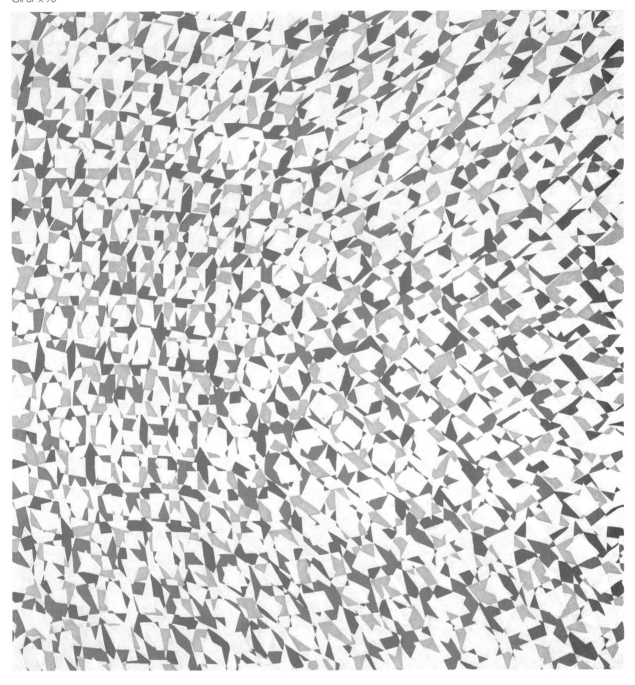

Peter Coker RA
London from Cranley Gardens
Oil 32 × 47

Peter Coker RA
Veules Les Roses
Oil 15 × 30

Michael Andrews
Oare, the Vale of Pewsey
Oil 72 × 84

Amanda Faulkner
Mangas and the Ghosts
Etching 14 × 16

Roderic Barrett
Burial Party
Oil 48 × 58

John Keane
Economics and Bananas
Screenprint collage 55 × 43

Kenneth Draper RA
Overlay
Oil and pigment on wood 40 × 46

Arthur Neal
Mrs Sweeney's Funeral
Oil 36 × 35

Anselm Kiefer

Yggdrasil

Emulsion, acrylic and lead 87 × 75

Flavia Irwin

Geomorphological Exploits 3

Acrylic 36 × 60

Leonard Rosoman OBE, RA

Peyton Skipwith and Edward Bawden

Gouache on paper 17 × 20

Kiow Ngor Ng
The Birth of Ideals
Intaglio collage 41 × 28

Kiow Ngor Ng
The Birth of Ideals
Intaglio collage 41 × 28

Elizabeth Adeane
Sheep and the Tree
Oil on board 16 × 23

Sally Hunkin
Winter Journey
Etching 17 × 22

Jennifer Percival
Dead Cypress Tree
Oil 7 × 7

James Rushton
Doppelgänger
Watercolour and body colour 11 × 9

Ken Howard RA
L'Udinesi
Oil 47 × 24

Sonia Lawson RA
Dancers
Oil 68 × 78

Eileen Cooper
Which, What, Why
Oil 48 × 48

Michael Rooney RA
Natural Histories
Oil 23 × 17

Norman Adams RA
The Deposition
Oil 69 × 49

Michael Buhler
Attraction of Opposites
Oil 35 × 24

Mary Fedden RA
Black Teapot
Oil 34 × 29

James Butler RA
Sleeping Child
Bronze h 4

Ralph Brown RA
Suzannah, Head
Plaster for bronze h 14

Phillip King CBE, RA
Abstract Fire King Number 4 (Diploma Work)
Bronze h 37

Megan di Girolamo
Mother and Child
Fired clay h 22

Installation shot of Gallery X

Suad Al-Attar
Once Upon a Time...
Oil 10 × 13

Simon Garden
Four Years Passed (No. 1)
Acrylic and oil 43 × 56

Henry Kondracki
The Red Park
Oil 86 × 78

Michael Hopkins CBE, RA
Holyrood with Amphitheatre
Model 36 x 20

Hampshire County Architects
Aldershot Park Primary School
Model 44 x 22

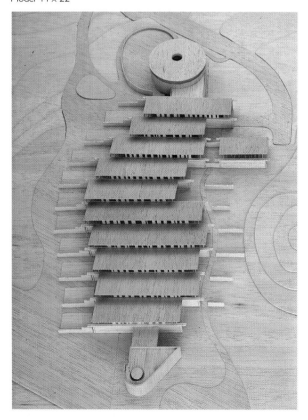

Sir Philip Dowson CBE, RA (Arup Associates)
Manchester Olympic 2000 Amec Stadium
Model (detail) h 30

**Installation shot of Gallery I with Michael Kenny RA's
'Francesca's Plight' in foreground**

Mimmo Paladino
Il Respiro Della Bellezza XI
Oil 80 × 80

Frederick Cuming RA
Morning Glory
Oil 40 × 50

Rita Smith
The Studio
Watercolour 23 × 31

Susan Hawker
Gardens No. 2
Oil 48 × 48

Anthony Eyton RA
Early Morning, Pushkar
Oil 15 × 25

Paul Ritchie
North Buchan Coast
Etching 11 × 14

Caroline Frood
Untitled
Acrylic 59 × 79

Edwina Leapman
Blue Painting
Acrylic 60 × 48

Jennifer Durrant
From a Distance
Acrylic 99 × 125

Anthony Fry
Nude in a Red Tent
Oil 66 × 73

Derrick Greaves

Falling

Acrylic oil collage 66 × 66

Derrick Greaves

Falling

Acrylic oil collage 66 × 66

Ben Levene RA
Glitz
Oil and silver leaf 21 × 27

Kyffin Williams OBE, RA
Snow Above Nant Peris
Oil 30 × 49

Jean Cooke RA
Dove with Garden
Oil 24 × 24

Terence Bennett
Street Scene, Scarborough
Oil 9 × 11

Joe Tilson RA
Apollo Pythion
Screenprint and woodcut 44 × 44

Michael Rothenstein RA
Sunset Bird
Woodcut 24 × 24

John Ward CBE, RA
Sir Peter Crill, Bailiff of Jersey
Oil 40 × 38

Norman Hepple RA
Fishing for Tiddlers
Oil 19 × 23

Sir Geoffrey Jellicoe RA

Landscape Plan for Denbies, Dorking, Surrey

Pencil 23 × 31

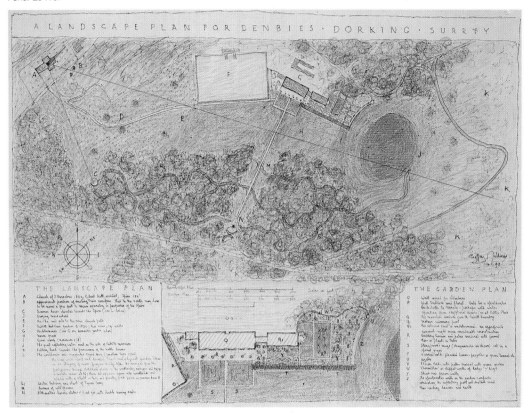

Jennifer Dickson RA

Diana the Huntress (Malmaison)

Hand-tinted etching 14 × 21

**Detail of the commemorative installation of works by
the late Dame Elisabeth Frink DBE, RA in Gallery III**

Sir Roger de Grey KCVO, PRA
Marennes Canal
Oil 49 × 39

INDEX OF PLATES

Jasper Johns painting on page 39 has been kindly loaned to the Summer Exhibition by The Eli and Edythe L. Broad Collection, Los Angeles.
A number of sculptors exhibiting in The 225th Summer Exhibition have kindly given permission for their work to be touched by visually impaired visitors.
These pieces are indicated in the galleries by a series of raised labels, and the list of works can be collected from the Ticket Office or Reception Desk on arrival.

Exhibits photographed by John Riddy and FXP Photography. Catalogue co-ordinated by Abbie Coppard and Nick Tite.
Designed by Esterson Lackersteen. Page makeup by Spy. Origination by DawkinsColour. Printed and bound by Watmoughs (Holdings) PLC

ROYAL ACADEMY OF ARTS IN LONDON 1993

THE ROYAL ACADEMY TRUST

Charitable Donations to the Royal Academy

The Royal Academy Trust was founded in 1981 to receive, invest and disburse funds given in support of the Royal Academy of Arts. Between 1982 and 1988 over £6 million was raised by public appeal: £4 million for endowment and £2 million for essential capital works. In 1989 the Trustees launched a campaign to raise the funds for major improvements to facilities at the Academy including the construction of the Jill and Arthur M. Sackler Galleries. A total of £10 million has now been raised for this capital project. The next phase of essential work to improve environmental conditions and renovate the Main Galleries has begun with Galleries I and II and fundraising for this and other urgent work is now underway.

Apart from this essential capital work, supporters of the Royal Academy may give assistance either by contributing to the Endowment Fund or by making a donation for a specific purpose such as the Royal Academy Schools, the Library, the educational services or the conservation of works of art. The Royal Academy welcomes legacies which may be for its general charitable purposes or be identified with a particular project.

Further information on charitable giving to the Royal Academy may be obtained from Griselda Bear, Director of the Royal Academy Trust (direct line: 071-494 5697) or from Kathrine M. Ockenden, Executive Director, American Associates of the Royal Academy Trust, 17th floor, 12 East 49th Street, New York, NY 10017, USA.

Corporate Membership Scheme

The Royal Academy offers companies the opportunity to join its highly successful Corporate Membership Scheme. Members receive substantial discounts on entertaining and priority booking. Other privileges include concessionary admission for employees, exclusive Private Views and loans of works of art for company premises. Annual subscription: Member £5,000 plus VAT, Associate £2,500 plus VAT.
Details are available from the Manager: 071-494 5704 (direct line).

THE FRIENDS OF THE ROYAL ACADEMY

Patron HRH The Duke of Edinburgh KG KT
Chairman Sir Roger de Grey KCVO PRA
Co-ordinator Susie Dawson

Further information from:
The Friends of the Royal Academy of Arts, Piccadilly, London W1V 0DS
Telephone: 071-494 5663/4

Friend

£35 annually plus joining fee*
Free and immediate admission to all Royal Academy exhibitions with a guest and children under 16 (to a maximum of four)
Discount on exhibition catalogues
Access to the Friends Room at the RA.

Private Views: the Summer Exhibition by invitation and otherwise on production of a valid membership card
Receive RA, the quarterly arts magazine
Other special benefits including lectures, concerts, tours

Friend (Dual or Family)

£50 anually plus joining fee*
A second membership card for two people

living at the same address which also admits guest and children under 16

Friend (Concessionary)

£26 annually plus joining fee*
All the privileges available to Friends
Those aged over 60, living more than

75 miles from London, aged under 26, Students (with NUS card), Disabled, Museum employees and Teachers are eligible

Artist Subscribers

£50 annually plus joining fee*
All the privileges available to Friends, plus three free forms to submit works to the Summer Exhibition
Discount on artists' materials

* Please note: A £5 joining fee is payable unless you pay by Direct Debit.
Gift subscriptions are exempt whatever form payment takes. Rates apply until 30 September 1993

Contributing Friend

£150 annually. In addition to the privileges of a Family Friend, invitations to special evening Private Views, to the first Private View for the Summer Exhibition, complimentary guest

passes and a complimentary copy of the catalogue and illustrated souvenir of the Summer Exhibition

Associate Sponsor

£25 annually. In addition to the privileges of a Contributing Friends, receive additional invitations to Private Views, three

complimentary exhibition catalogues of your choice annually, and listing in the Annual report and exhibition catalogues

Sponsor

£750 annually, which may be paid under Gift Aid. In addition to the privileges of an Associate Sponsor, receive a complimentary catalogue for each exhibition (the hardback

edition where available), viewings before the galleries open to the public, the privileges of a Library visitor, and reciprocal privileges at certain major art galleries abroad

KEW GARDENS
Gallery

The Specialist in Botanical Painting

Mary Grierson's
'Flowers from Around the World'

JUNE 11 - AUGUST 30 1993

PAINTINGS FOR SALE

Royal Botanic Gardens, Kew, Richmond, Surrey TW9 3AB
Telephone 081 332 5618

Society of Wildlife Artists
30th ANNUAL EXHIBITION 1993

The Mall Galleries
The Mall, London SW1 (near Admiralty Arch)
29th July to 13th August
Open every day 10-5 pm
Admission £2 Concessions £1

The Patricia Well
Galler

Morton House, Lower Morton,
Thornbury, Bristol BS12 1RA.
Tel: (0454) 412288.

"Welsh Valley Nr. Merythr Tydfil" Oil 24"×20"   by Judy Strafford

We specialise in the Promotion through
Advertising and Exhibitions the Advancement
of Artists to a larger purchasing public

AUTUMN EXHIBITION 1993
Sat 16th October to Sat 6th November

THE THAMES THROUGH LONDON, TREES AND FLOWERS
Paintings by **GILLIAN WHAITE**
29th September to 10th October 1993

Museum of Garden History, Lambeth Palace Road, London SE1 7JU 071-261 1891

he Thames Barrier   *Oil on canvas 30" × 40"*   *Gillian Whaite*

THE SUMMER EXHIBITION – a unique open forum for all expressions of ART, selected by a discerning Committee and presented as a rare and stimulating spectacle of diverse talents.

"SUMMER AT FORTNUMS"

A seasonal presentation from THE DEPARTMENTS OF FORTNUM & MASON, selected by discerning connoisseurs of good taste and presented to you daily from 9.30am (except Sunday). A unique experience in itself, unanimously selected and Internationally acclaimed, and reflecting the diverse attractions of its own Culinary Galleries ...
THE PATIO, ST. JAMES'S AND FOUNTAIN RESTAURANTS in PICCADILLY.

FORTNUM & MASON

181 PICCADILLY · LONDON W1A 1ER
Tel: 071-734 8040 · Fax: 071-437 3278